Amrita Sher Gil

A PAINTED LIFE

Copyright © Rupa & Co 2002
Text © Geeta Doctor 2002

Published in 2002 by

Rupa . Co

7/16, Ansari Road, Daryaganj
New Delhi 110 002

Offices at:
15 Bankim Chatterjee Street, Kolkata 700 073
135 South Malaka, Allahabad 211 001
PG Solanki Path, Lamington Road, Mumbai 400 007
36, Kutty Street, Nungambakkam, Chennai 600 034
Surya Shree, B-6, New 66, Shankara Park,
Basavangudi, Bangalore 560 004
3-5-612, Himayat Nagar, Hyderabad 500 029

ISBN: 81-7167-688-X

Paintings courtesy: The National Gallery of Modern Art, New Delhi &
Photographs of Amrita Sher Gil courtesy: Vivan Sundaram

Cover & Book Design by
Arrt Creations
45 Nehru Apts, Kalkaji, New Delhi 110 019
arrt@vsnl.com

Printed in India by
Gopsons Papers Ltd.
A-14 Sector 60
Noida 201 301

Amrita Sher Gil

A Painted Life

Geeta Doctor

Rupa & Co

CONTENTS

CHAPTER ONE

A Sensualist of the Eye

In her life, as in her work, Amrita Sher Gil attracted instant attention. From the moment she stepped into the crowded canvas of the Indian sub-continent in the early 1930s, she sparkled with all the exotic allure of her half Indian-half Hungarian parentage. In a society that was in the grip of the powerful currents of change, struggling to transform the old colonial-feudal order to meet the demands of the 20th century, Amrita leapt gracefully over the breach keeping intact her equilibrium. In her own way using a devastating array of weapons–intelligence, wit, warmth, but most memorable of all the aura of beauty–she celebrated the arrival of the individual. It was accompanied by an ardent search for a more just and egalitarian system of values, particularly in the country that she had decided would be her own canvas—India. Amrita was able to stamp her own personal quest for self-expression as an artist into an unrelenting search for the soul of the yet unborn nation.

She plunged into the Indian landscape drinking in the colours, with orgiastic glee. "How can one feel the beauty of a form" she asked, "the intensity or the subtlety of colour, the quality of a line unless one is a sensualist of the eyes?"

She reminds one of the American poetess Emily Dickinson, who, filled with the same heightened sensibility, could exclaim: "An inebriate of air am I,/And debauchee of dew,/ Reeling, through endless summer days/ From inns of molten blue." It is as if in recording a moment of pure sensual pleasure, the eye itself becomes drunk, the tongue learns to see and the self dissolves into a dizziness of delicate colours.

Or as Amrita would add, "And art, not excluding religious art has come into being because of sensuality: a sensuality so great it overflows the boundaries of the mere physical."

Leaving behind her years of formal education at the Ecole Nationale des Beaux Arts in Paris, Amrita returned to her family estate, near Amritsar in 1934, to begin what was to be her own journey of discovery. She was twenty one years old at the time. No one knew that she had only seven years ahead of her. In that short span of time, she seemed to traverse many worlds. Through her canvasses, she breathed in the Tahitian air of a Paul Gauguin, tasted the apples set on a table by Paul Cezanne, tumbled with the rough peasant contours of Van Gogh's Arles, filling the outlines of her figures with the tenderness of the portraits that she found at Ajanta, while at the same time dipping her feet in the warm waters of the Indian Ocean on her journey to the South of India. She challenged the landscape of the Indian imagination with her men and women who gaze out and away from her canvasses willing us to look at them again, and yet again.

Looking back on her brief, but brilliant trajectory, through the misty dawn of the Indian art world in the thirties, she appears like a small green emerald breasted, hummingbird plundering the nectar from the throat of every brilliant flower that it encounters on its path. Small-boned, bright and bejeweled in brilliant silks and long dangling earrings, Amrita herself would hover just for an instant in the air, before tearing into the heart of yet another lover, another argument, or more importantly, another subject for a painting. She

Bride's Toilet. *Oil on Canvas.*

mastered the contradictions that made her the restless creature that she was by transmuting them into the watchful stillness of her luminous compositions. Just as she managed to transcend her dual inheritance as aristocrat and artistic outsider into a triumphant act of ownership that made her, the first, the most celebrated, as also the most fiercely debated of artists, to herald the modern age of art in India.

"India belongs only to me!" she declaimed with all the hauteur of the privileged autocrat. At the same time, she also reminded herself that she had a mission, "I am personally trying to be, through the medium of line, colour and design, an interpreter of the life of the people, particularly the life of the poor and sad. But I approach the problem on the more abstract plane of the purely pictorial, not only because I hate cheap emotional appeal and I am not, therefore, a propagandist of the picture that tells a story."

CHAPTER TWO

Hungarian Rhapsody

Even if she had not become the acclaimed artist of modern India, Amrita's life had the romantic quality of a gothic tale, which began long before she appeared on the scene.

Amrita's father, Sardar Umrao Singh Majithia was very much an aristocrat whose family owned large tracts of land, near Amritsar, given to them by Maharaja Ranjit Singh. They had fought bravely on the side of Maharaja Ranjit Singh, against the British. In the next round of battle, the Majithia family fortunes suffered gravely. This time, they found themselves on the losing side, fighting against the British, who took their lands and banished the head of the family to Benaras. During the Great Rebellion of 1857, however, Sardar Umrao Singh's father was loyal to the British. As the head of the Majithia clan he was reinstated and given the title of Raja. He was also awarded a large area of land in the Gorakhpur District of U.P.

After his death, his two young sons were made the wards of the British Government. While the older one inherited the title and was to remain very much a loyalist to the ruling side, Sardar Umrao Singh, after an early arranged marriage and the death of his first wife, went to the London. It was here that he met the young daughters of Maharaja Duleep Singh, the youngest son of Maharaja Ranjit Singh, who having been sent into exile, became a part protégé of Queen Victoria.

According to Amrita's biographer, N. Iqbal Singh, the "handsome young Sikh aristocrat" as he describes Sardar Umrao Singh, was a tremendous hit with one of the princesses, the princess Bamba. When he left for India, she decided that it would be a good time to visit the ancestral home of her parents. Princess Bamba, chose as her travelling companion on the long journey back India, Marie

Amrita Sher Gil in Paris.

Antoinette, a well-educated and cultured Hungarian woman who was trying to find a footing in London. The fact that she was an accomplished musician made her the ideal companion, since Princess Bamba was also fond of music. Not surprisingly, when Umrao Singh went to pay his respects to Princess Bamba, his eyes fell on the vivacious companion, Marie Antoinette, whose flaming red hair was to capture the imagination of all those who met her. The handsome young Sardar was no exception. Particularly, since she was sitting at the piano and singing, tossing her splendid head of hair, no doubt, as she entertained Princess Bamba's friends at an evening of classical music.

From that moment the compact between the high-spirited Hungarian pianist and the quiet Sikh aristocrat was sealed. They were married in 1912, at Lahore, according to Sikh rites. Even after Maharaja Ranjit Singh's time, Lahore continued to assert its power as the intellectual and cultural capital of the North. It boasted of a cosmopolitan culture, unlike Amritsar, that remained for the Sikhs in particular, their spiritual centre. Soon afterwards, the couple left for Hungary where they were to live during the war years. During this period, the nationalist movement was gaining force in India and Sardar Umrao Singh, who was suspected of having made contact with some of the leaders, found it difficult to get back. It was ten years before he could return with his young family to India.

Despite the hardships of wartime, they were to be some of the happiest years in the life of the young couple. Amrita was born a year after their marriage, on the 30th of January, 1913. She was "a

beautiful baby with silky black hair reaching down to her neck and big eyes that seemed to survey the world with astonishment," recalled her mother while her father noted her broad forehead. Already, watching tenderly over her infant's cradle, her parents had taken sides, one choosing beauty as her guardian, the other, intelligence. The next year there was another baby, Amrita's sister, Indira.

Musicians. *Oil on Canvas.*

In the early years of her life, Amrita lived with her family in a country house, outside Budapest, surrounded by scenes of rural life, whose colours and shapes she drew in the childish scrawls of her first pictures. From the earliest time, she also had her cousin, Victor Egan, as a close friend and confidante. He was her aunt's son, on her mother's side. Their childhood friendship was to survive the changing emotional allegiances of young adulthood, when each of them moved away to find new friends and different interests and the often, long separations, when the Sher Gil family left for India. In her deepest self however, Amrita remained connected to her childhood experiences of the Hungarian countryside and her cousin Victor. Perhaps, she had always known that she would marry him one day, even though by the time she got around to it, she was famous. Even Victor had his reservations, wondering whether she would be content to be the wife of a struggling doctor. Her mother was crushed. She belonged to a generation that believed that the only purpose of cultivating a young woman's talent and beauty was to make a splendid marriage.

When Amrita was a little older, the family moved to Budapest where they lived in the style that Marie Antoinette felt would be more suited to bringing up her daughters. The contrast between the countryside and town, between village and city, between the rural ideal of a simple style of life and the all too obvious attractions of a metropolitan culture, was to be another dominant aspect of Amrita's dual inheritance.

Quite apart from her flaming hair, Marie Antoinette had an equally remarkable passion for music, which she passed on to her older daughter Amrita, who played the piano with a fervent intensity, particularly when she was under the grip of any strong emotion. Her mother dearly hoped that her daughter would become the concert pianist that she had once aspired to be. That both her daughters were exceptionally talented was of course, taken for granted. They were raised with the expectation that they would be star performers, preferably in the world of music. After that, each would make a splendid match, in keeping with their aristocratic background. Like one of those folk tales from central Europe, where the specially chosen child always shows a streak of stubborn self-will that will take her away, further and further, from the expected path, Amrita was to both justify her mother's expectations for a glorious life and also to frustrate them at every step.

Amrita was a gifted musician and a precocious child who had a fondness for language. Very early, she decided that the one language that she could really enjoy was the language of colours. As she said, "It seems to me that I never began painting, that I have always painted. And I have always had, with a strange certitude, the conviction that I was meant to be a painter and nothing else."

As Victor Egan remarked much later, "She showed every sign of becoming an artist, because in an amusingly childish way, she would draw or paint on any bit of paper that she could find, even on a torn envelope or any scrap of paper she could lay her hands on. She would paint on the walls. The house used to be littered with her drawings, She was never interested in a black pencil; it had to be coloured. The pictures she often drew were of funny looking

creatures, some looking like human beings."

Maybe, it was the imprinting on her infant mind of her mother's crowning glory of red hair that instinctively sharpened her response to strong colours. Her mother recalls singing Hungarian folk songs to her that she would immediately illustrate. Or she would tell her the typical bedtime stories that Amrita went on to draw, eventually creating her own small word pictures. It's interesting to ask whether the artistic impulse is inborn in a person, like Amrita, or whether it has to be nurtured. Iqbal Singh records Victor Egan as saying, "She decided to become an artist at a very young age, and under no influence, because her mother was more interested in music. She had absolutely no understanding as regards painting and art. I would rather say that she was more or less against it, because she ridiculed modern painting, which she found distorted or ridiculous. She got no encouragement from the parents. Her father, who was an orthodox Sikh, could not understand modern painting at all. To become a painter was entirely her decision. She wanted to, and intended to, and insisted on it."

Malcolm Muggeridge was an Assistant Editor on the staff of *The Statesman* at Calcutta, in 1935, when he met the Sher Gil family during his trips to Simla, which was as he noted, "an authentic English production; designed by Sahibs for Sahibs". This was where the Sher Gils had their personal family retreat that they named, *My Holme* at Summer Hill. It is here that Amrita held court, in the Season, attracting in turns, the more urbane and intelligent of the Englishmen, of whom Muggeridge was a prize catch, as well as

Siesta. *Oil on canvas.*

Self Portrait. *Oil on canvas*

the ardently nationalistic Indians who were to become the new intellectuals of young India. No matter how much she flaunted the "Indian" side of her parentage, there's no doubt that with every step that she took, she had to make a choice. Her extreme and often intensely felt convictions must have been a reflection of the contrasts imprinted in her genes and the tensions of living in a home dominated by two persons, with very strong and opposing views of the world.

As Muggeridge recorded in his diary, his initial reaction to Madame Sher Gil, as he called her, was one of contempt. Showing signs of the acerbic style, that was to make him the crusading critic of his time, he dismissed Madame Sher Gil as being a "triumphantly vulgar woman" whose flaming red hair, only served to underline Muggeridge's fastidious but somehow typically English distaste of all foreigners. For as he remarks, "Madame Sher Gil's whole style of living—bourgeois Viennese in the days of the Austro-Hungarian

Empire transplanted to Simla of all unlikely places—was displeasing to him (her husband)." About Sher Gil's father, Sardar Umrao Singh, Muggeridge has left behind an equally vivid portrait of a Tolstoyan figure, with a long beard and flowing shirt fastened in the middle with a belt, in the manner of a Russian peasant. According to Muggeridge he spent his time evading his wife's attempts at gracious living by contemplating philosophical matters, or by escaping to the terrace, where he could watch the stars.

"Up on the roof by night, he was a wild-looking figure, hair and beard disheveled in the wind, peering intently through his telescope as though he hoped thereby to get nearer to the stars and their celestial music…"

His views on Amrita, that he recorded in his diary, ranged from initial fascination at her exotic charm to the total

Young Girls. *Oil on canvas .*

21

surrender of the besotted lover. He met her for the first time, at Simla's fashionable Hotel Cecil. "I danced with the Hungarian-Indian several times, made her promise to ring me up…she is very sensual and made-up, was wearing an exquisite silver and black sari, is self-consciously arty; has studied in Paris. We danced! I said I'd like to dance till I swooned. She said that she'd never swooned, but that she supposed I had!" For a young woman of a mere 22 years, Amrita exhibited all the poise that her Parisian conquests had given her on the sexual front.

Her comments about Muggeridge show that what she was looking for was intellectual stimulation. She is almost breathless in her description of her conquest when she writes to her sister. "I have met an extraordinary Englishman," she says. "He is really one of the most interesting, fascinating, remarkable people I have ever met. I have never met anybody like him. (This feeling is entirely reciprocated.) And among this dull uninteresting and scandal-mongering crowd, we are an intense relief to one another." She ends, on a slight note of triumph, as she murmurs in French, that aside from Muggeridge, she has made several other conquests that season, all of them very facile victories. Muggeridge on his part is quite chaste in describing his side of the consummation of their love

Hungarian Village Market. *Oil on canvas.*

affair. "Now there was perfect harmony between us" he records. "I explained to Amrita how she was really a virgin, because she never experienced the spiritual equivalent of copulation… She had many lovers but they had left no scar." As though to underline the "spiritual" nature of their romantic tryst, he also records that they spent the evening "together under a tree in the moonlight and riding back, the road white and the trees black, and the mountains shadowed, I felt exhilarated." This, from a man who had earlier been highly critical of Amrita's tendency to exaggerate each one of her encounters with her former lovers by reading out aloud from old love letters, in an impassioned voice, speaking in French like one of Colette's coquettish heroines, shows the extent of his capitulation.

After the first few meetings, she invited Muggeridge to her home and showed him her paintings. His response is somewhat cool. "They were not commonplace," he remarks, "but how good they are I can't be sure. At the same time she's got a touch of genius." By this time, Amrita had made him the ultimate compliment. She wanted to paint him!

The portrait of Malcolm Muggeridge is at the National Gallery of Modern Art, New Delhi. It shows a youngish man, somewhat formally encased in layers of gray-brown material, shirt, tie, waistcoat and jacket, that merge into the almost monochrome background. He sits wedged against a wall, reclining on a sofa or a bed, perhaps, looking somewhat gauche and awkward. His eyebrows raised in what could be described as a quizzical, slightly mocking look, accentuate the triangular planes of the cheekbones and strong pointed chin. There is a tenderness about the eyes, just as the skin is also given a muted amber glow. His right hand is shown limply signaling the trademark of the working journalist and elegant lover-he holds a bone-white cigarette in a slim black cigarette holder.

What is interesting is to see how similar the pose, the stiff awkwardly held body and the extended right hand, with the long fingers extended, the thumb half hidden, as though she did not yet know how to wedge the thumb to the hand,

Malcolm Muggeridge. *Oil on canvas.*

25

is to an earlier portrait that she had done of a dearly beloved artist friend of hers at Paris—Marie-Louise Chasseny, three years earlier, in 1932. Even the eyebrows and prominent chin are the same, and it is interesting to recall that when she was writing to her sister about her first impressions, it was to compare Muggeridge to the friend whom she had most admired during her art school days, Marie-Louise. Whereas the portrait of Marie Louise Chasseny is in the realist mode, with strong colours outlining the heavy lips and skin tones, her study of Muggeridge shows her looking at him, more distantly as a series of signs, or fluid shapes that flow into an easy rhythm.

The strong lines that contain the figure, only to be erased so that the image merges with the background, suggest that like the semi-transparent envelope that the writer Virginia Woolf sought to create around her characters, Amrita was interested in searching beyond the image of the person that she had before her. It should be kept in mind that this was an era, when there was a great deal of speculation about the soul, about auras, about matter dissolving into atoms leaping about from one field of energy to another, and all the myriad theories uncovered by the different schools of psychoanalysis regarding the many splendoured facets of consciousness.

This is particularly true of Paris, where the attempts at an alternate style of living by adherents of a Gurdjieff, or an Ouspensky, attracted kindred spirits, like the young writer from New Zealand Katherine Mansfield, who stayed at Fontainbleu with just such a group. There were stunningly new experiments in dance and choreography by the Russian émigrés, who had fled the Revolution, that liberated the body and clothed it in the light shimmering fabrics, that the industrial revolution was making available. As the yearning for political freedom was beginning to make itself felt in Asia, Africa and South America, artists, poets and writers, shared their often radical views in the heady atmosphere of Paris between the Wars.

The East was believed to be the repository of ancient wisdom. Any person garbed in the flowing robes that marked the magician, as well as the seer from the East, was accorded complete attention and there is an amusing story of how Sardar Umrao Singh, walking in the Bois de Boulongne on afternoon was accosted by two young Indian students who believed that he was a fakir, only to be taken in his chauffeured car to his elegant apartment, to meet the family. Amrita must have been well aware of such claims. It is only to be expected that she too would be drawn into a search for the nebulous quality that would link all experiences into one luminous image, a stream of pure awareness, representing the universal mind.

In the Muggeridge painting, Amrita has allowed herself to experiment with the space around the sitter, suggesting a considerable amount of skill in handling the background and

Women (1938). *Oil on canvas.*

foreground with an imaginative use of detail that adds greatly to the composition. Muggeridge himself was to write about the experience of being painted by Amrita. Whether he is writing about it from hindsight, or whether he finds himself reduced to an "object" in the predatory gaze of the artist and hence rejected by her, Muggeridge now describes Amrita entirely in the terms of "an animal sensuality".

He notes that she paints him with a kind of ferocious hunger, sweating while she works. After she has finished, he says that she falls back in complete exhaustion at her efforts. Or as he was to write in his memoirs, *"Chronicles of a Wasted time—The Infernal Grove"* where he goes back to the subject of her painting. "It was this animality which she somehow transferred to the colours as she mixed them and splashed them on the canvas."

CHAPTER THREE

The Parisian Interlude

Once Amrita had decided that she wanted to be an artist and nothing else. Marie Antoinette rose to the challenge. Only the very best would do for her daughter. Already, on their return to India from Hungary when Amrita was still just a small girl, not yet ten, they halted en route at Paris and had a look at the famous works of art at the museums, for which the city is so well known.

While they were in Simla, Marie Antoinette made sure that she found the best art teacher that she could find. Major Whitmarsh, the first one who undertook the grave responsibility of training the future artistic prodigy, did not last long. He insisted that she practise repeatedly at creating an exact likeness. He was soon dismissed. Her next teacher, Bevan Petman was a portrait painter, who had great popular success undertaking commissions for the well-known society ladies of Simla. Not just that, having been a teacher at the prestigious Slade School of Art in London, he was more than competent in instructing his still very young student. As he was to say to Iqbal Singh in a letter, written almost five decades later, he could recall Amrita with all the clarity of a teacher, who recognized an exceptional talent.

"It soon became apparent that she loved this business of expressing three-dimensional form on a flat surface with a pencil. She worked so hard, unremittingly, without pause for I think she felt that this was something she could learn and desired passionately to accomplish. It was extraordinary how quickly she learned to express form with only a single line, and I soon realized that I had in my hands a rather unusual not to say remarkable little person, who, if allowed to might well become a real artist. She readily understood what I told her and soon knew what she was trying to do. She was happy with me, and I grew extremely fond of her and gave her all I could."

Finding the right mentors was always a necessary part of Amrita's progress as an artist. Equally, when she found that the atmosphere was too rigid or stifling as she discovered on the occasion when her mother decided that a spell in Florence would instill in her daughter the essentials of the Italian art of the Renaissance, Amrita dug in her heels and revolted. Fortunately for her, Marie Antoinette for once listened to her daughter, now all of eleven years and took her out of the strict atmosphere of he Roman Catholic School at Florence. It would not be out of place to add here, that both Amrita and her sister had been baptized into the Roman Catholic Church, during their infanthood in Hungary. This did not however incline them to any kind of religious orthodoxy.

Amrita was however charitable enough to say, when she was old enough to look back at her brief sojourn in Italy, "Unconsciously though, my stay in Italy was to affect my artistic development later. It is there that I conceived a liking for Italian Masters of the Renaissance, which later towards the middle part of my stay in Paris was to manifest itself in my manner of painting. This tendency elicited from somebody at the time that I was a 'descendant of the great Venetians'. " It is evident that even an apparent failure can be transformed to a triumph when projected through the eyes of someone who knows that she belongs amongst the "greats". Amrita always managed to sound completely sure of herself as though she were serenely and completely in control of her life. The truth was somewhat different. She had to battle against lack of appreciation and, even worse, a complete lack of understanding of her attempts to break through the barriers that made so much of Indian art weak and sentimental—two attributes that she rejected with a passion that made her seem arrogant. It only sharpened her own response to her work crating in her an almost fanatical desire to impress her vision upon the world.

After the failure of the Florentine project, Amrita returned to Simla, where her parents tried to persuade her to join a good convent school, like any other girl of her age might have done. Again, Amrita rebelled against the strict rules of the institution, this time actually managing to be expelled, since she professed to have become an atheist.

Again, she was supported in her decision to continue her education at home, by her parents. They allowed her to paint and sketch and draw, while learning music. Since her father was at that time interested in translating the verses of the Persian poet, Omar Khayyam, her paintings reflected turgid scenes in the dreamy Omar Khayyam mode. This could explain why Amrita so often turned upon the dim witted votaries of the Bengal School, as they were

known, for their vapidly romantic paintings that looked to the past to create a pastiche of what could pass for national glory. The sentimental strain is one that lurked quite closely in her own backyard and she knew that she had to fight against its languid embrace every time that she as an artist, who was also a woman, took up her brush.

Besides Simla, the summer capital of the Raj, the Sher Gil family also stayed at Saraya, near

Haldi Grinders. *Oil on canvas.*

Gorakhpur, U.P. with members of the extended clan. It was here, that many years later, at the family estate near the village of Saraya, that Amrita was to paint some of the most vivid of her outdoor compositions. Since, she had also been drilled in the importance of drawing from life, the availability of sturdy village women and peasant men with strong features and a monumental quality in their moments of repose, allowed her to make them pose for her at her whim. These ties to rural India, feudal and emotional, were an important feature of her artistic life. Because of her family connections, she had easy access to both Saraya and to the Majithia household near Amritsar, as well as to her parents' own comfortable home at Simla.

Fortunately for her, Ervin Baktay, an uncle from the Hungarian side came and spent some time with the Sher Gils in 1927. He immediately recognized the unusual quality of Amrita's youthful compositions. He was an artist himself, who had achieved a fair degree of success until one day he recognized that since he would never reach the heights to which he aspired, he might as well give up the task and turn to other interests. Amongst these, aside from the study of languages (he was fluent in 22 different languages from around the world), Ervin Baktay became a well known Indologist and scholar of Tibetan studies. His views would appeal to both

Marie Antoinette and Sardar Umrao Singh. Ervin Baktay lost no opportunity in persuading the Sher Gils to allow Amrita to pursue her artistic career in Paris. He would arrange for the necessary introductions to be made, through his network of Hungarian artists, who knew Paris well.

After some initial resistance, Sardar Umrao Singh decided to follow his advice. The whole family would shift to Paris. They arrived in the Spring of 1929. Amrita was readily accepted at the Grand Chaumiere, under the tutelage of Professor Pierre Vaillant. She was sixteen at the time. Her professor was frankly astonished by her ability and took her immediately under his wing. For a young artist whose models until then had always appeared sheathed in many layers of cloth, the opportunity to work at life studies was exhilarating. Amrita learnt more about the human body in all its fleshy and bony contours than she could have hoped. Her drawings and paintings were not any different from those of any other student, but they were an important part of her understanding of the human anatomy.

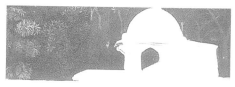

None of the later work of her Indian period exposes more than the face, the hands and the feet of her figures. The exception perhaps is the highly ritualized composition of young Brahmin priests from South India, sitting together like glossy aubergines and raw bananas, but she still manages to suggest the corporeality of those brides waiting

The Ancient story teller. *Oil on canvas.*

on their string beds that she painted, much like the nude figures that she had taught herself to understand in her Paris days.

Before the end of the year, Amrita had moved on to another well-known institution, the Ecole Nationale des Beaux Arts, and an even better teacher, Lucien Simon, who was well known as an artist of the Post Impressionist phase. The break had come because she had suffered an attack of appendicitis and needed an operation. There was some hesitation about her getting into the Ecole des Beaux Arts since she was as yet under age, but Lucien Simon was impressed enough with her work to agree to take her as his pupil in his studio. It was complete bliss as far as she was concerned. For as she described it, "Lucien Simon never 'taught'. He made us think for ourselves and solve technical and pictorial problems ourselves, merely encouraging each of those pupils whose work interested him in his or her own individual self-expression." She found the atmosphere of being left alone to solve her technical problems on the canvas very much to her liking. She "never avoided difficulties". She confesses, "I have not only welcomed them but have gone out of my way to look for them, and this characteristic has always been the principal feature of my nature and has manifested itself in the precociousness of my artistic development."

Paris also liberated her as a person. It celebrated the feminine and the dusky Eastern sensuality that she seemed to exude with every

Camels. *Oil on canvas.*

39

glance of her dark eyes, abundant black hair and full red lips, as can be seen from the number of self-portraits that she did in this period. Paris was in the grip of a worshipful discovery of "negritude" where any form of "otherness" signified a return to a more primal and therefore elemental order of life. African art, African forms were being imitated and studied for their vitality and tremendous purity of form.

Simplify! Simplify form, colour, shape, even ideas, and get to the essence of things—that appeared to be the prevailing fashion. Or as Amrita explains it, what she is trying to do in her paintings, is to avoid painting pictures that tell a story, but look for "the abstract yet vital plane of line, colour, form and design…" She wanted to move away from the studied fussiness of her parents' well furnished apartment on the Rue Bassano, with its 18th century French furniture and floors covered with Oriental carpets, to the simplicity of the bohemian life that her fellow students promised her on the streets of Paris. It was a lesson that Amrita was to absorb, even as she learnt to speak French with a freedom that only underlined the freshness of the other freedoms that she had decided was her birthright as an artist.

Despite her mother's best efforts to introduce her to Parisian high society by taking her to the concerts, the opera, and the theatre, where top hatted and gloved companions would see that her precious daughter was given the recognition due to a "Princess" from the East, Amrita fled from her charmed family circle. She had more important matters at hand. She had to paint. She had to educate her eye with all the wealth of world art, particularly the art from the country which she already knew she would make her own. Only by looking at the pieces of ancient Indian art in the museums of Paris had she understood their value. They had stirred in her mind the resolve that one day, she would go out in search of those places that existed only as names, places full of a mythic grandeur that resonated in her mind with the names of Ajanta, Ellora, Tanjore.

As was her nature, or maybe just the impetuosity of youth, once she made up her mind she could only state it in extravagant terms. "I know for certain," she claimed, "that had we not come away to Europe, I should perhaps never have realized that a fresco from Ajanta, or a small piece of sculpture in the Musee Guimet, is worth more than the whole Renaissance." Her parents should have recognized what this change of artistic allegiance was leading to, but they could not imagine that their daughter, who seemed to be such a success in Paris, had now decided that her place was actually in India.

As Amrita wrote, "towards the end of 1933, I began to be haunted by an intense longing to return to India, feeling in some strange inexplicable way that there lay my destiny as a painter." She was encouraged in this by her professor Lucien Simon who observed, "although sad to part with a much loved and talented pupil, (I feel), that her virile art and powerful sense of colour would have greater scope of expression in India than in the dull gray atmosphere of the Paris studio." It is interesting to note here, that her professor was one of the first to notice the 'virility' in her work. The conflicting elements of a masculine gaze that sought to be balanced by the more overtly obvious feminine aspect of Amrita's personality, is part of the tension that she struggled to

Alfred Cortot. *Pastel on paper*

43

confront in her work. In today's terminology it would be called engaging the two sides of the brain.

For Amrita's family, the decision to return to India was met with dismay. They were well aware of her numerous romantic liaisons, though they may not have known that her escapades had serious consequences, as on one occasion, when she had to take refuge with Victor in Hungary and ask for his help in getting an abortion. Indeed, she accuses her father for not wanting her to go back to India because he was afraid that her "reputation" would spoil the good name of the family. "I was rather sad," she writes to him "to realize that you place the conservation of your good name above your affection for us. I don't in the least consider myself an immoral person. I am not immoral. Never was in the true sense of the word (which however but few people understand)".

"I wish to return primarily in the interest of my artistic development" she went on to tell her father on a more professional note. "I now need new sources of inspiration and here you will perceive Duci, (Father), how utterly mistaken you are when you speak of our lack of interest in India, in its culture, its people, its literature, all of which interests me profoundly and which I wish to get acquainted with, and I think I will find it in India."

Three Girls. *Oil on canvas.*

Describing the difference in the method of approach between the West and the East, Amrita observed that in Europe she "had been painting in the purely Western, in fact almost academic style, placing the stress principally on the execution, which was considered to be extremely brilliant," As she goes on to add, "The moment I put my foot on Indian soil not only in subject, spirit, but also in technical expression my painting underwent a great change, becoming more fundamentally Indian. I realized my real artistic mission then: to interpret the life of Indians and particularly the poor Indians, pictorially; to paint those silent images of infinite submission and patience, to depict their angular brown bodies, strangely beautiful in their ugliness; to reproduce on canvas the impression their eyes created on me; to interpret them with a new technique, my own technique that transfers what might otherwise appeal on a place that is emotionally cheap, to the plane which transcends it and yet conveys something to the spectator who is aesthetically sensitive enough to receive the sensation."

The differences in atmosphere and style can best be seen in two works that Amrita did, one of them at Paris, the *Young Girls* painted in 1932 that won for her a much coveted recognition, the honour of being elected as an Associate of the Grand Salon of Paris in 1933, the other on her return to Simla—*"Three Girls"* that she painted in 1935. In the first case, not only is the setting European with its stylish boudoir atmosphere but there is a stiff formality about the composition. There are hints that Amrita has been looking at the methods of some of her favorite artists like Cézanne, references to whose still life compositions appear in the table in the right foreground, and in the plate of fruit that is being held by the woman on the left. There is also evidence of an influence of the Italian artist Modigliani, whose elongated nose appears in the same woman's, somewhat melancholy oval face, and even to Renoir, the French artist whose portraits of fair young women may find an echo in the pale alabaster skinned girl, who is combing out a veritable cascade of blonde hair. The use of white in all its tonal variations-of skin, hair, frothy nightdress, diaphanous undergarments with broderie Anglaise, a white comb held in one pale hand, the white satin slipper on one foot, the creamy Lily of the Valley in the vase that stands on a small table covered with a white cloth and the bleached wood of the upholstered chair-reveal the skill with which Amrita had mastered the Western model. She is completely at home in it, and yet seems to keep her distance.

Amongst the series of paintings in 1935, after returning to Simla and setting up her own atelier here, Amrita worked steadily at a number of compositions, including of course, as described earlier, the portrait of Malcolm Muggeridge. Her paintings of *Hill Men* and *Hill Women* seem to echo the colours of her European palette. They explore carefully massed shapes in vertical figurations, with the faces turned in profile, full front and glancing away, as in the portrait of the *Young Girls.* The colours are all grays and browns, the very tones that she had used to paint a scene of the streets of Paris

Resting. *Oil on canvas* .

from her window. It is fascinating to recognize that one of the veiled women in *Hill Men* who is shown seated on the ground, has an elongated hair-style covered with a length of transparent white cloth, that is very similar to a study by Paul Gauguin of a woman wearing a cloth bonnet in his 1888 painting *The Sermon after a Vision*. For some reason, the hands of her Hill Men and Women are all but obscured by their long draperies.

It is interesting here to speculate very briefly on the influence that Amrita might have absorbed from her father's fondness of photography. It has been well documented of course that as the photographic image invaded the public sphere, it changed the way in which artists began to look at the world. The closely cropped views, the slightly elevated angle looking down upon the scene, rather than straight towards it, and since these were still the days of black and white photography, the sudden impact of white to enhance the sense of mood and atmosphere, must have played a part in developing Amrita's eye. Particularly since many of her father's pictures were engaged in documenting his daughter's life.

Be that as it may, the most spectacular of the paintings done in 1935, has to be the one entitled *"Three Girls"*. All the lessons in colour and form have been assimilated now in one rich harmonious composition that is so evenly balanced that it does not reveal its

secrets easily. It is both dramatic and refined. The shadows behind the three young women hint at the uncertain future that might well be ahead for them, yet they gaze into it with a steady, even a calm acceptance, that is not exactly resignation, not an elated anticipation, but a certain preparedness that comes with knowing their role in a large plan of things. Perhaps the word should be rootedness. Amrita, the celebrated traveller in different worlds, but eventual exile in all of them, could well be envious of the inborn belief that so many of her men and women have in her paintings a sense of being of the earth, and from the earth, almost elemental beings, who get their strength and tremendous sense of poise from knowing that they belong. In their own way, the *Three Girls* were wide-hipped and indicative of the fecundity that earlier societies rooted in the uncertain rhythms of nature, worshipped in the splendid Yakshis, or nymphs of the trees and forests. Amrita may not have been aware of these sculpted female figures, though she was to fall in love with the Mathura sculptures when she did finally see them. It is more than likely, that she would have seen Modigliani's own warm and voluptuous nudes, arms raised above their heads offering themselves up for consumption, just as she must have known his chunky tree-like figures and caryatids carved

Sitting Nude. *Oil on canvas* .

Self Portrait.
Oil on canvas.

out of stone. Her figures have the same kind of solidity, made incandescent by a growing confidence in using colour.

Quite apart from anything else, the deep reds, the vermilion, the burnt orange of the background merging in the darker browns of the skin tones, the ripe mango complexion of the first young woman, the Gauguinesque emphasis on their sturdy village woman's hands, and the trademark use of white tones to balance all the hectic reds and oranges, show Amrita triumphant. She said that she had to return to India, because of her intense love of colour. Here, with all the flamboyance that her nature could unfurl at will, together with the iron discipline that she had learnt during her studies, Amrita was to proclaim her independence. This was what she meant when she said that India was hers and hers alone. She had conquered it from within. She had arrived.

CHAPTER FOUR

Brightness at Noon

"You know, there are two selves in a man." explained Amrita to Prem Chand, a student of philosophy in Delhi. , while he was sitting for her, at her request in her studio at Simla. She was trying to tell him that though the artist in her found him full of interest, as her second self, the woman, she was not in the least bit attracted to him. Though she did not say so to his face, the real reason that she needed to paint him was that she found that "his face was so ugly that it fascinated me!" When he asked her why he could not be part of her inner circle of friends she explained in no uncertain terms why this could never be. "Here I am an artist; you fascinate me as an artist. But as a human being, I have no place for you. As a human being, I enjoy my life. In that there is dancing, there is drinking—in drinks there is only beer and champagne for me; no other drink—and there is my own sex life...In that kind of life, you have no place." In the tersest manner, she had told him that for her purposes he would have to be content in being small beer. To another one of her admirers, she put the matter even more briefly. "Art is my business not Heart," she said. This kind of independent attitude was to make her something of a puzzle to several of her male friends, who were alternately attracted to her apparently easy ways and repelled by her equally brisk rejection of their company. One of her more perceptive friends was to remark that, "she hungered for awareness not power. And her great delight was to share this awareness with another human being. Sometimes it seemed that she projected some of her own awareness on to the people she liked just so that she had the joy of sharing it. Her close friends felt that her very presence made their own awareness sharper and their senses quicker." He added that even her sensuality that was to become the stuff of legend amongst the various men, who after her death boasted of having been intimate with her,

"was a means to the end of getting to know and understand people... to observe people in the throes of intense emotion." As for herself, he said, "She had that hard core of the artist that keeps itself aloof and untouched."

Meanwhile her work was attracting a certain amount of attention. Her *Self Portrait* won a prize at the All India Fine Arts Society. Here too, the picture that she had painted of Prem Chand, entitled *"Man in White"* was thought to show an achievement on the part of the artist that the judges felt was a "remarkable success". At the 46th annual exhibition of the Bombay Art Society her painting of the *Three Girls* won the Society's Gold Medal.

This was by far the most significant recognition of her talent. She was received with much acclaim at Bombay. Several papers interviewed her. It was also her first meeting with Karl Khandalavala, art historian and propagandist for the new age of modern art that was just beginning to dawn. He was one of the judges on the committee of the Bombay Art Society and Amrita, who needed an informed critic and intellectual peer was only too glad to turn to him.

"I admit I am not yet above the desire for recognition and success,"

Bride. *Oil on canvas.*

she wrote to Karl, "and because I had more or less given up hope of them by refusing to cater to public taste or pandering to the ideals of exhibition committees (never dreaming that there could be people like you in their numbers) it has come as a double pleasure to have gained recognition by adhering to my ideals. I am grateful to you for this."

She had already made herself something of a sacred monster by returning a prize given to her by the Simla Arts Society. Her comments on the feebleness of the artists belonging to the Bengal School were now beginning to sound like a drum beat of a challenge that could not be ignored. As she wrote in an article in *The Hindu* pointing out that most of these artists were churning out "so called paintings that depict an India where the Sun shines with an inevitability that was only equalled by the mediocrity of the conception and execution of that sunlight as it plays on flesh tints of standardized gray browns and give an opportunity to the ambitious artists to exploit the possibilities of orange 'reflected lights' and 'blue-light' (cheap tricks of the trade that have to be learnt but must be forgotten before one can even think of producing true works of Art)... These portraits of beggars, of the miserable, the poor of India, viewed as objects of topographical interest, without an atom

Resting (1939). *Oil on Canvas.*

of either artistic or human understanding."

As against this artistic twaddle, as she explained it, she was on a new track. Or to quote from her article, she added, "I am an individualist evolving a new technique that, though not necessarily Indian in the traditional sense of the word, will yet be fundamentally Indian in spirit. The eternal significance of form and colour interprets Indian and principally the life of the Indian poor, on the plane that transcends the plane of mere sentimental interest."

She was throwing the artistic gauntlet down in no uncertain terms. What gave her the new confidence was that not only did she have people like Khandalavala, with whom she could share the problems that she set herself in each one of her paintings, bouncing off ideas, borrowing some of his own insights and creating the dialogue that she knew was most important to her intellectual development, she herself was on her trip of discovery through the great artistic centers of the past.

At the same time, she admitted, "Although I have studied, I have never been taught painting in the actual sense of the word, because I possess in my psychological make-up a peculiarity that resents any outside interference. I have always, in everything wanted to

Woman at Bath. *Oil on Canvas.*

find out things for myself." Writing at this time, she was to add, "I am deviating more and more from naturalism towards the evolving of new and 'significant' forms, corresponding to my individual conception of the essence of the inner meaning of my subject."

Her journey to the South was therefore very much part of a search for a new and 'significant' form that would convey all that she had assimilated since coming back to India. Her visit to Ajanta exceeded all her expectations. She wrote to Karl, "I made a number of little drawings of Ajanta and Ellora and have learnt a lot." She was to return repeatedly to the cave paintings, describing Ajanta as "vibrant, subtle and unutterably lovely". At last she exclaimed, "I have for the first time since my return to India learnt something, from somebody else's work."

She explained why exactly she became angry when she found those artists who said that they admired the art of Ajanta, had actually stopped short of understanding it. In a letter to Karl, she wrotes. "It is because there are many possibilities in Indian art that I am literally opposed to those that have not explored these possibilities and decry those who have misunderstood it so profoundly."

On the other hand, when she stopped at Hyderabad and met Sarojini

The Swing (1940). *Oil on canvas.*

Naidu, her immediate response was to report in one of her letters, "I have met a wonderful woman at last—Sarojini Naidu." She was less than flattering about the then legendary art collection of Nawab Salar Jung, who was equally cold towards her, returning her pictures with the remark that he had no use for her "Cubist pictures". She was to find the same polite rejection from other members of the southern royalty. This was more than a source of irritation to her, not because she had expected anything different, but because by now the need to make some money from her work was beginning to haunt her. "Funny," she said after her diplomatic faux pas in pointing out the utter feebleness of the Nawab's art collection, "that I who can accept a present without the least pang of conscience, should not say that a bad picture is good, even if it is in my interest to do so."

As she went further south to the famous temples of Madurai and Rameshwaram what fascinated her the most were the people who visited these places. Contrasting the fantastic colour combinations worn by the Tamil people, with the predominantly white garments worn by those at Trivandrum, now known as Thiruvananthapuram, she wrote to her sister in early January 1937, "The people, men, women and children are extraordinarily beautiful. The women wear a bodice and a dhoti, leaving the middle portion of their body naked. They have a wonderful way of doing their hair, so that it stays without aid of a single hair-pin in a low enormous bun at the nape of their neck. The men (some of them have long hair too and wear a bun at the back! One would think it was ridiculous till one saw it) are naked except for a dhoti. Both men and women wear white exclusively, and I tell you the general impression is fascinating. Imagine a background of rich emerald green vegetation, coconut palms, banana, all the large leaved decorative trees one sees in the paintings at Ajanta...." The colour green was to be one of her favourites, appearing in pieces of clothing, as the background and as the luxuriant foliage in a tropical country, particularly in symbolic representations of a solitary palm, or tree shape after her visit to Ajanta.

Her response to the other places on her Southern itinerary, the Padmanabhapuram Palace, the paintings on the walls of the Mattancheri Palace at Fort Cochin, which were relatively unknown at the time, are equally vivid and full of enthusiasm.

When she reached Cape Comorin, she was able to do a sketch of Gandhiji during one of his prayer meetings. She was also able to paint. She described one of them as "a largish composition, a woman with two children on an apple green background" in which she had painted the figures in dark red and raw sienna and clothed in white. As she wrote, "I am fairly satisfied with it. I feel I have assimilated Ajanta to some extent." This is amongst some of the best loved of Amrita's works, which form part of the paintings that she was to create after her Ajanta trip, that show her trying out the lessons that she had absorbed during her long journey. The painting that she called *Fruit Vendors* is also known as *Banana Sellers*.

There is a fluid plasticity in her style that captures the soft roundedness of her little South Indian family sitting on the reddish earth, with their nominal bunch of bananas by the side. The utter ordinariness of the moment is transformed by the artist's gaze into a life enhancing experience that touches not just the three figures sitting there, but the viewer too, who is drawn by the movement of the brown and white forms against the living breathing background of tender banana leaf green and banana flower red earth, into a sense of a "being-in-oneness" with the subject. The dark oval faces, the angled head of the figure on the right, that is shown in near profile, with eyes aslant and the hair drawn back into an exaggerated knot at the back of the head, the prominence given to the whites of the eyes, or just in the earrings worn by the mother from her pendant ear lobes, show that Amrita has mastered some of the aspects of the Ajanta murals, especially their dramatic use of white. Even the manner in which the trio of banana sellers waits patiently by the roadside, looking up expectantly towards an event that just might happen ahead of them, is reminiscent of the figures of ordinary people seen waiting for the moment of enlightenment in a traditional fresco painting. Certainly, the flower that the young girl on the left holds in her hand, the ardent glow that lights up her face, suggests that even a very ordinary life can have its moment of transcendence.

In a later work done at Saraya in 1938, there is another family group that she called, *Women* where again she has used the figure of a young girl, who appears in the midst of her heavily veiled and draped relatives, like a cut-out from an earlier age. She is shown naked in all the innocence of youth, her hair decorated like one of the young princesses from Ajanta, her eyes heavy lidded and half closed in wonder as she looks at one crimson flower that she holds, like the fresco image of Padmapani, in her hand. This along with paintings such as *Elephants Bathing in a Pool* and *The Verandah with Red Pillars* as also the one that shows a woman stepping on a swing show her playing with the different modes of painting, besides Ajanta-the Pahari paintings, with their rich colours, the Mughal miniatures with formal use of structure to suggest multiple viewpoints and the Rajasthani ones for their celebratory mood to indicate the passage of the seasons, if not the vitality of life. As she was to write about them; "These little compositions are the expression of my happiness and that is why perhaps I am particularly fond of them."

It is as though the intense concentration of effort that she needed to compose the trio of paintings that are regarded as the fulfillment of her vision made it possible for her to indulge herself in a more playful mood. The three paintings of her mature style, done soon after she returned from her epic journey to the South are *The Bride's Toilet, Brahmacharis,* and *South Indian Villagers Going to the Market.*

It is interesting to hear what Amrita herself has to say about the colours that she used in the *Bride's Toilet* since she is so precise in explaining her vision. It was, she explained, a long composition, the horizontal spread perhaps a reflection of the murals that she had just seen. "I have defined and made more compact the breast of the fat woman on the right and have also defined the upper portion of the woman's body on the extreme left, worked on the hands and feet of the child on the extreme right and in short greatly improved on the colour scheme" she wrote.

"The fat woman's skirt which is an unexpected greenish yellow lights up the whole picture. The little girl in the middle is clothed in a crimson cloth with white circles, her face and body are a sort of ivory colour. The woman doing her hair is a rich burnt sienna with reddish orange in it, her skirt is a warm peacock blue, her blouse acid green with purple sleeves, the pot's pink, the whole background and foreground a grayish ochre more or less of uniform

Brahmacharis. *Oil on canvas.*

Amrita Sher Gil in Shimla in 1937.

colour…. (rather varied in brushwork though.) The kid in the centre is a deep brown with occasional green tinges and the child on the extreme right is as though lit up by a flame…"

Obviously, this only provides some idea of the inner workings of the artist's mind in using those elements that she always said excited her the most, colour. It gives no idea of the limpid timeless quality of the finished portrait, which illuminates the ivory skinned figure of the bride into an almost iconic image. Her oval face and tender limbs belong to the androgynous image of the Buddha as well as certain representations of the young woman, who was to become the Madonna. Equally, her glance, the wet tendrils of her hair that drip down her bare back could well be the regal composure of one of the princesses taken from the frescoes on the ancient murals of the caves and temples that Amrita had just seen.

Is there resignation in the calm stillness of the women who have gathered around the young bride, in a ritual that seems half sacrificial, as the body is prepared for the offering that will affirm her entry into the deepest mystery of life, the continuation of the life force? Or is there in the gorgeous array of colours and rounded limbs, breasts, pots, half filled containers of vermilion pastes and unguents, a suggestion that this is a celebration, a joyous and conscious surrender to an event that every girl must desire?

There are no answers obviously either to the enigma posed by the Bride and her helpers, or to the equally majestic study of the five young *Brahmacharis* sitting close together, their hands raised or held stiffly by their sides in some ballet-like movement the artist places before her audience. The *Villagers Going to the Market* that belongs to the same period is less complicated. Here, it is relatively easier to see the resemblance to the movement of people crowded together in a common purpose, wearing very distinctive styles of clothing that may be noticed in some of the frescoes at Ajanta. The bodies are elongated, the faces appear like in the African inspired sculptures of the men and women of Benin, with long limbs and heraldic faces shaped like shields. This is equally true of her Brahmacharis. They look quintessentially South Indian, and the very essence of the refined priestly type, but it is just as well to remember that Amrita, who could not paint unless she had a model in front of her, has used her North Indian watchman as the main character in the picture.

As she wrote to Karl Khandalavala about the "Brahmacharis", "My chief object in painting this picture (by the way the most difficult thing that I have ever attempted, I have yet to know whether successfully) was uniformity, a *leitmotif* of forms and postures. Although I have brought a variety of colour in the flesh tints, the figures from left to right are deep green, orange brown, light yellowish, burnt sienna and ochre colour respectively, they don't disturb the calm of the picture. (I was anything but calm, though, while I was painting it! I scratched the head of the central figure about six times and struggled and struggled before I got it as I wanted it.) Not to speak of the rest! But don't you think that on the whole, I have learnt something from Indian painting and sculpture?" Amrita answered this question in her characteristic manner by immediately moving on to another style, another mode of representing reality, by painting the smaller compositions of the elephants and "women" that have already been described. Her characteristic restlessness was also beginning to make itself felt. She decided that the time had come to make a trip to Hungary and honour her long-standing promise to get married to Victor, which she did on the 16th of July 1938.

For some time at least, it seemed as though Amrita was happy with her decision. The couple lived in the countryside, but with the war clouds looming over Europe, they too torn with the uncertainty of deciding whether to stay in Hungary, where Victor had to follow his army unit, working as a doctor, or whether to leave for India. Despite being separated from him and having to live on her own quite often, she managed to keep her mind busy with ideas. She had re-discovered Breughel and the painting that

she named, *Hungarian Market Scene* is in the mode of Breughel, full of bustling figures and activity in the front, dominated by a tall white sided Church at the back. It is a sombre painting, with small veins of colour breaking through in the dark corners where the carrots and apples that are being carted to the market, spill out on the ground. A painting called *The Merry Cemetery* is set against the same dark and gloomy landscape, but it is almost cheerful in the prospect it offers of tilted crosses and gravestones that have been painted in bright colours, while yellow daffodils and a red tulip bloom from the graves.

Despite these attempts at keeping her spirits up, Amrita was deeply disturbed to hear from her parents that they had, in a bid to protect her future reputation, destroyed all her correspondence. Some of these letters were from famous people, there was for instance a six-page letter from Jawaharlal Nehru, an admirer of hers who had visited her exhibition at Delhi and observed that what he particularly liked was her ability to combine both strength and perception. She on her part had told him that he had the ability to look at her paintings without seeing them, a distinction that she often made, when she felt that people were responding to her work only through their intellect.

The Merry Cemetery. *Oil on canvas.*

As she wrote to her parents; "I must admit it was a bit of a shock to hear that all my letters are being perused and destined to the flames! I had already destroyed a whole roomful of letters some weeks before my departure. Those letters I specially kept either because they were dear to me, amused me, or were important from the artistic point of view or otherwise... I merely hope at least the letters of Marie Louise, Malcolm Muggeridge, Jawaharlal Nehru, Edith Lang and Khandalavala, have been spared. I had left them behind not because I thought them dangerous witnesses of my evil past but because I didn't wish to increase my already heavy luggage."

She continued to paint, while following her husband around, as she told Khandalavala, like a "good Indian wife to where he is stationed for the time being". Her paintings of *The Potato Peeler* a very robust study of a girl working at a kitchen table, her face and hands an almost hieratic emblem of the dignity of labour and *Two Girls* a virtually black and white study of two girls posed somewhat stiffly by the side of a bed, show her exploring European themes in a manner that best suits them.

It must have been a relief for Amrita to return to India with her husband. After the long sea journey that took them to Sri Lanka or Ceylon, as it was then known, and then by gradual stages to the temples of Madurai and then onwards to Madras, where they visited Mahabalipuram, travelling in a horse drawn carriage over dry river beds and streams until they reached the deserted spot, which Amrita felt was "the most haunting place in South India" they finally arrived by way of Delhi, to Simla. Amrita painted the charming composition of a woman resting her head on a heavily embroidered bolster, with one arm supporting her head, half asleep, half watching a child wearing an elaborate peaked cap being held by a servant woman, almost as if to reassure herself that the world of Pahari miniatures, where such women did indeed spend their time *"Resting"* (as she called her painting) was accessible to her.

Artistically, it was to herald a new phase of work when Amrita settled down at Saraya once more, this time with Victor who had been assigned as Doctor-in-charge of the Majithia Estate Dispensary. This time it is her interest in the Mughal miniature tradition and some of the other schools of Basohli and Kangra miniatures that fires her imagination, as in *"The Ancient Story Teller"* and *"Haldi Grinders"*. There are the open air compositions that she paints by carefully marshalling her repertoire of models and animals around the landscape of Saraya as in *"Elephant Promenade"* and *"Camels"*- the last one seems to borrow the language of the artists of Bikaner. There are scenes of intimate laughter and play that reflect the

77

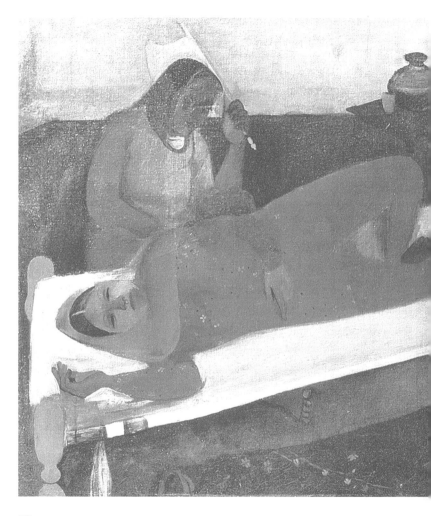

Rajasthani miniature style as in *The Swing* and *Village Girls*. There are also compositions such as *Woman on a Charpoy* and *Bride* where all these traditions merge into one dramatic image that goes beyond the immediate subject matter to attain a clarity of purpose and execution that shows her to be in perfect control. It was to be a prolific phase, but already the need to find a more stimulating environment was making itself felt. Though she had the chance to make a few trips outside of Saraya, one of them to Benaras with Khandalavala, these did not hide the fact that both she and Victor were marooned in a provincial backwater.

They decided to move to Lahore. Amrita had immediately adapted herself to making a home for herself that would reflect her artistic temperament. Victor occupied the ground floor for his clinic. Their apartment became a natural meeting place for discussions on art and literature. She was what would be described now as a celebrity and her views on art and almost every other subject were sought after on the radio and in the local press.

Woman on Charpoy. *Oil on canvas.*

She loved entertaining people at her house for tea, recalls her husband, who adds, "Amrita, basically, was interested in people. She was extremely critical and selective, but she got a tremendous enjoyment out of meeting people whom she liked, or whom she considered sufficiently cultured or interesting."

Amrita had planned to have an exhibition of her work at Lahore towards the end of December. She started work on a scene that she could observe from her window. It looks a little cramped and the view it affords is of the

Red Varanda. *Oil on canvas.*

buffaloes that were being raised by her neighbours, but this does not seem to hamper her new method of composition, using the multiple planes that the miniature artists had taught her so well. In the midst of all this planning, Amrita suffered what appeared to be a sudden hemoerrhage. To this day, there are no clear accounts of what might have caused it. One of the images that remain is that by the time her friends arrived, she lay pale and waxen, in the midst of "blood soaked sheets".

Her last words were about colour. She was looking at the sunlight, the last rays of the evening sun soaking through the curtains of her bedroom, creating patterns on the wall, swirling colours of blues and reds and greens that she could still feel about her eyes. Even as she struggled to remember them, identifying the different colours by their names, she fell into a coma. On the 5th of December, the same evening, close to midnight, she quietly breathed her last. She was only 29 years old.

As Emily Dickinson might have told her:

We never know how high we are
Till we are called to rise,
And then, if we are true to plan,
Our statures touch the skies.

Chapter Five

Touching the Skies

Amongst the many portraits that remain of her, two of them show her in two very distinct poses and frame of mind. They are just two of the many self-portraits that she did. One of them painted in the manner of Paul Gauguin, shows her with her body turned towards the viewer, a lushly endowed young woman, offering herself, rich red lips, open hair spread out in cascading abundance, the skin flecked with tinges of bronze-gold, neck and arms banded with beads and bracelets. Not surprisingly, she herself has subtitled it 'The Tahitian'. She is presenting herself, as the world wanted

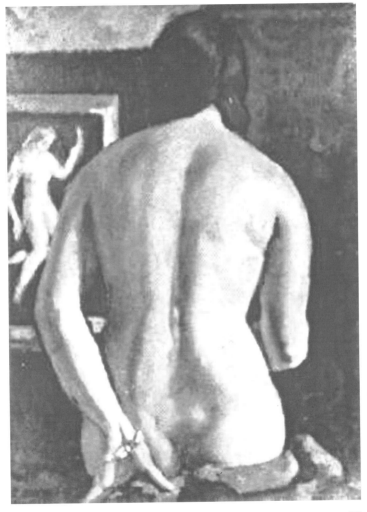

her to be, an artist caught in the male gaze, even if she is the one doing the looking, but not so much as an artist, as much as a beautiful woman. This was painted in 1939, at the height of her fame.

The second one was painted earlier, in 1932, her student period. It shows her sitting at her easel, in front of a window, with the light streaming towards her body from the left, in a more serious mood. She is severely dressed and though there is still the suggestion of sensuality in the soft roundedness of the body, it is a very hard, almost cold glance that she is directing at herself, (and the viewer), in the act of painting. The painting arm itself is muscular and strong and suggests that the heavy 'manual' work involved in painting.

It reveals the many contradictions that Amrita encountered in the course of her short life. There was the question of her beauty, or perhaps it was not a question at all. It was simply taken for granted that anyone aspiring to be a woman and an artist had to be sensuous and languid, preferably doomed, in the manner of the pre-Raphaelites who had set the tone for such matters with the women they celebrated on the canvas. Many of the women that the Impressionists used as their models, for the apparently languid and aristocratic beauties stretched out on their chaise longue, were actually maids, washerwomen, prostitutes, young women who still had the scent of fresh hay of the countryside on their bodies as they tramped the streets attempting to make a living in the cities of the recently industrialized world.

Amrita added to the ambiguity of her role as artist and woman, by reversing the equation. She was undeniably aristocratic. By underlining the sensuality inherent in her work and of the image she presented to the world, she created an aura so highly charged with sexual energy that she seemed to blast open the way ahead with an almost invincible force that she knew beyond doubt was the truth. Her images of Brides, tensely draped in red, their ripe bodies stretched out on string cots, dangerously angled inside

closed rooms, her processions of dark silent figures waiting for a sign, were as much a passionate reflection of her own search for meaning, as of her desire to look as deeply as she could into the lives of the people, whom she once felt she could illuminate through her art. It is as if part of Amrita's power lay in being the archetype of a maiden, the vestal virgin of male imagination, who had to pay the price of entering the till then privileged world of artistic creation controlled by men, with images that contained in them hints of a bloody chamber that confirmed the worst fears of a feudal patriarchy-of the female force rampant that was exemplified in the case of Amrita by her own sexual history.

As the same time, there are compensating arguments that reassure the curiosity of the public that "To Amrita, sex was an expression of her sensuality, and sensuousness in her was a necessary concomitant of the creative urge." "It seldom" we are told by Amrita herself, "upset her emotional equilibrium." Because, 'she could fall out of love, or fall in love with someone before any damage could be done." Further, that she "indulged her sensuality but was not a slave to it." Or "Said that she had a physiological peculiarity because of which she could go through the entire conventional pattern of physical sex without being emotionally affected herself."

Nude. *Oil on canvas.*

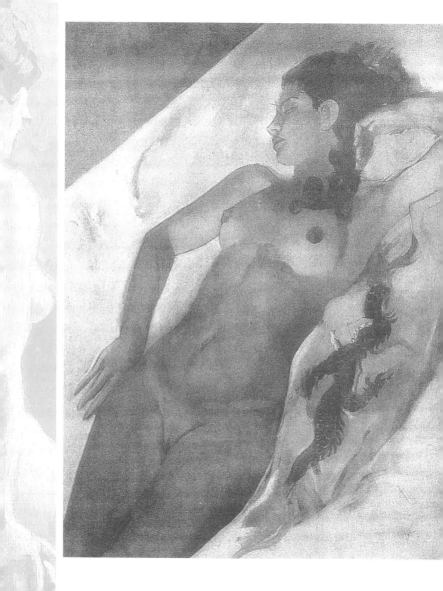

Two Women.
Oil on canvas.

No matter what methods she used, the artists who came after her could not afford to ignore her tough minded approach or her relentless search for a new mode of artistic expression that would take in the past, document the present while reaching out to the future.

What is equally fascinating is to note that unlike other women artists, Amrita preferred not to document her own physical body in all its 'peculiarities' if this was indeed the case or to claim the exclusive privilege of displaying it with a feminist point of view. Her paintings bridge the distance between the standard masculine gaze and her own feminine view that seeks to be a more compassionate equalizing one. Even while lying prone on her charpoy, waiting for the night to come, her red robed *Woman on a Charpoy* is given the essential dignity due to a human being. This rigour, this ability to detach herself from the immediate scene and render her subject in vivid forms and colours is perhaps another side of her hybrid vision. She can be both male and female, both Indian and European in her ability to stand aside and paint.

Finally, however what comes through is her honesty and plain speaking, "It's not that I am cleverer than others" she said, "It's that the others are stupid."

BIBLIOGRAPHY

Amrita Sher Gil - N. Iqbal Singh. Vikas

Amrita Sher Gil - Mulk Raj Anand. NGMA

Sher Gil - Baldoon Dhingra. Lalit Kala Akademy

From Expressions & Evocations -(ed) Gayatri Sinha. Marg

The Making of Modern Indian Art - Yashodhara Dalmia. OUP

The paintings of Amrita Sher Gil can be seen at the
National Gallery of Modern Art, New Delhi.

Self Portrait. *Oil on canvas.*

NOTES